DAM TROUBLE

By Frances Silberstein
Illustrated by Ned

We respect and honour Aboriginal and Torres Strait Islander Elders past, present and future. We acknowledge the stories, traditions and living cultures of Aboriginal and Torres Strait Islander peoples on this land and commit to building a brighter future together.

Library For All Ltd.

I sit on the edge of Mornington Dam near our farm, watching the lilies floating in the water.

Then, I see my two brothers getting ready to launch their raft.

They didn't tell me they were taking the raft out!

I decide to swim to them.

I leap up, run along the dam,
and land on the raft with a *thud!*

My brothers are not happy. They wrestle me until I fall into the water.

Luckily, I am a good swimmer and keep calm as I swim back to the raft.

But then it floats away, and
I get angry.

Suddenly, something long and slippery in the water brushes against my leg.

I scream. I'm so scared!

I think it's a big water snake. I call to my brothers for help and swim lightning-fast to the raft.

My brothers see me panic. They cheer me on and then pull me up on to the raft.

Then, we see ...

... a long, wet reed in the water.

Phew!

I'm safe. It's not a water snake after all.

What an epic swim, though!

You can use these questions to talk about this book with your family, friends and teachers.

What did you learn from this book?

Describe this book in one word. Funny? Scary? Colourful? Interesting?

How did this book make you feel when you finished reading it?

What was your favourite part of this book?

About the author

Frances is from the Whadjuk Nyoongar Nation of Perth, Western Australia. She loves playing games, eating yummy food, and being with family. As a child, Frances' favourite book was *The Rainbow Fish*.

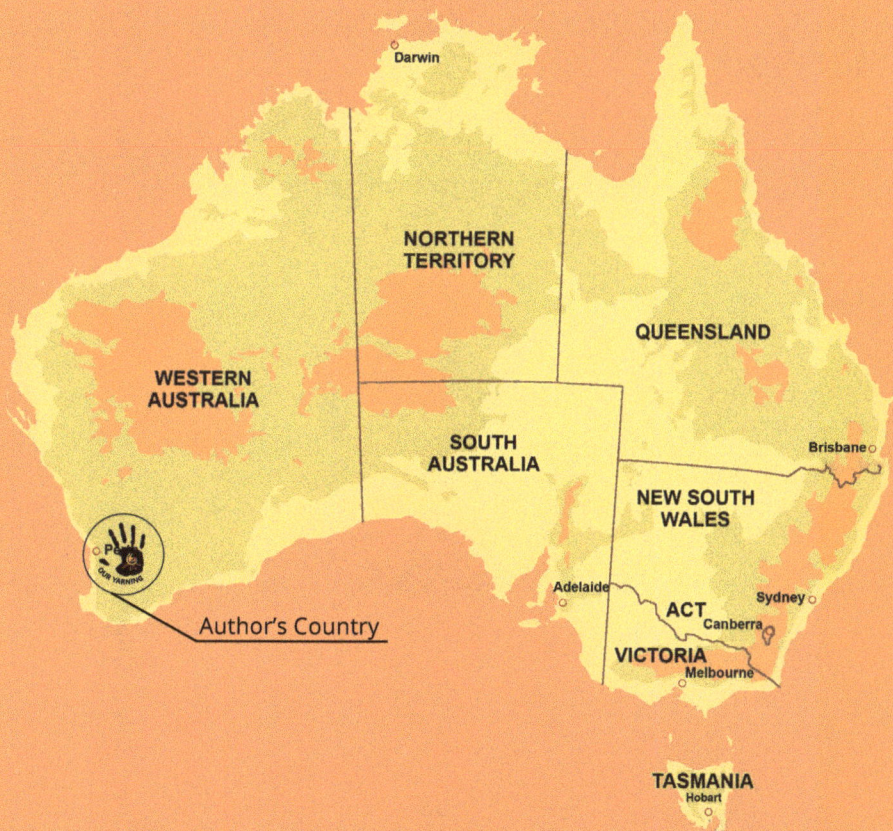

Darwin

NORTHERN
TERRITORY

QUEENSLAND

WESTERN
AUSTRALIA

SOUTH
AUSTRALIA

Brisbane

NEW SOUTH
WALES

Adelaide

Sydney

ACT
Canberra

Author's Country

VICTORIA

Melbourne

TASMANIA
Hobart

Our Yarning

The Our Yarning collection aligns with the Australian Curriculum through the Cross-Curriculum Priorities — Aboriginal and Torres Strait Islander Histories and Cultures. The collection provides an authentic opportunity for learning and embedding Aboriginal and Torres Strait Islander perspectives because it is written by Aboriginal and Torres Strait Islander people.

We know that children learn better, and enjoy reading more, when they see themselves in the stories, characters and illustrations of the books they read.

To download the app, visit the Google Play Store on any Android device and search 'Our Yarning'.

You're reading Level 3

Learner – Beginner readers

Start your reading journey with short words, big ideas and plenty of pictures.

Level 1 – Rising readers

Raise your reading level with more words, simple sentences and exciting images.

Level 2 – Eager readers

Enjoy your reading time with familiar words, but complex sentences.

Level 3 – Progressing readers

Develop your reading skills with creative stories and some challenging vocabulary.

Level 4 – Fluent readers

Step up your reading skills with playful narratives, new words and fun facts.

Middle Primary – Curious readers

Discover your world through science and stories.

Upper Primary – Adventurous readers

Explore your world through science and stories.

Dam Trouble

First published 2024

Published by Library For All Ltd
Email: info@libraryforall.org
URL: libraryforall.org

Our Yarning logo design by Jason Lee, Bidjipidji Art

Original illustrations by Ned

Dam Trouble
Silberstein, Frances
ISBN: 978-1-923143-98-2
SKU04321